Loving Yourself:

It's An Inside-Out Job

By

Kareen Borzone

When I first met Kareen Borzone in July 2018, I was a middle age woman trapped, in thinking, I had to stay in a job that did not serve my needs or reward me for the work I had been completing over the past 25 years.

I allowed myself to believe, I was unworthy, not smart enough and insecure about the way I looked. I did not believe I could compete in an industry of insurance and financial service professionals. I allowed myself to stay in a job that had not provided an increase in salary over the last 10 years in spite of getting the highest performance ratings and training very highly effective individuals to become number one in their Market Areas outperforming the entire Enterprise.

When I first met Kareen, I thought, "how is this little woman going to tell me anything?" Little did I know, the giant was powerful! Kareen got me to open up and talk about things from my childhood that I had allowed to shape my adulthood. She helped me understand the story I had made up to survive, that no longer severed me. As she probed deeper into my life and my history, she assisted me to see how everyone in my life believed in me and loved me for who I am.

But if I did not love and believe in me, nothing else mattered and I would always be "Playing Small in MY LIFE!"

Kareen helped me understand, I could live my life allowing my circumstances to limit my beliefs and my abilities, or I could "choose and move" understanding I am lovable, I am worthy and I am enough. I chose the latter and I continue to choose. This powerful woman has shaped so many lives, through mindset and capability training. I am forever grateful. I was blessed enough to be in her presence.

Today because of Kareen Borzone, I choose to release fear and rejection and take action daily, to improve my life to understand my limiting beliefs so that I can work to improve the lives of others.

Kareen is a mentor who I highly respect! I only wish that I had a woman in my life much earlier who would be willing to tell me the truth and have me own my abilities, come and help me grow into womanhood. There is so much work to be done and I am so glad that she is a pioneer in this field for not only women but men and children as well!

Sandra Tatum – CEO
VP Global Marketing Inc
Sandra Tatum Enterprises LLC – (Consulting Services)
9821 Investments LLC – (Real Estate Investments & Development)

Table of Contents

Acknowledgments

To Lorraine, also known as My Mom, your unending Love continues to get me through tough moments in Life. Thank you for always believing in Me. Making you laugh will always be one of my most favorite things. You are truly my example of ALWAYS doing the Right Thing.

I Love You Mom.

To My Sisters, your willingness to hold up the mirror and point out my blind spots is invaluable. You allow me to see myself. You remind me that I Am Worthy and Valuable. My relationships with each of you continues to enrich my Life. You are the wind that allows my Super Cape to flap in the wind. I am Bigger and Better from knowing you.

To my John, what a journey we have traversed together. Thank you for providing me the space to experience ALL of Who I Am. You are the peanut butter to my jelly, the Vodka to my Tonic, the hot fudge to my sundae. Thank you for taking care of our Kiddos and our Home while I am away, working and living my Vision. Thank you for being my #1 Fan. Thank you for always having coffee ready for me every morning. Thank

1

you for teaching me what Laughter feels like. I love who I am when I am with you. I love you Honey.

To my Sachi and my Lulu, being your fur Mommy is one of the greatest Joys in my life. You really are the center of my Universe.

All My Love,

Kareen

CHAPTER 1:

Getting to Know Kareen Borzone

(Subira)

Hello, Everyone. I want to welcome you to the State of the Union. We've got Kareen Borzone with us today, and I'm so delighted about this. I am Sensei Subira Folami. My website is SenseiSubira.com. Today, I'm talking with Kareen, who is an expert on loving yourself. I can say that confidently and boldly because I know her story, and she is gracious enough to share this information with us. What I know to be true is you can teach what you've lived, and Kareen, you have lived some amazing experiences that I know have brought you to this place of loving yourself deeply today.

I have watched you in that process. I'm super, super excited about the women you will be empowering with your book through your story. You remind women that they are BIGGER than any life event they have lived through or may be in the process of moving through. Also, you remind women that they are BIGGER than any belief they may have held about who they are that has disallowed the full authentic expression of who they really are. What a gift that is.

I'm honored to hold this space with you today. I'm honored to be your student, while you share with me, and with the rest of the women who are reading your book, what life has taught you as you've sat at the feet of your own life and learned. There's no more powerful place to sit.

As it turns out, you're a well-known expert in understanding what you've done over the last 20 years. Your journey is inspiring and awesome.

I know many women ages 45 and older who want to know about the opportunities and the challenges we're living with today.

I have a few general questions about your background and experience in the field of loving yourself so women can understand who you are and where you're coming from. Then we'll jump into your thoughts around the State of the Union, according to Kareen, when it comes to loving yourself. This way, women can understand how to move forward, especially in times when we find ourselves stuck or hitting a plateau. Let's jump right on in.

(Kareen)

Alright, well, I am 50 years young. I am born and raised in Hawaii. I am the first grandchild on both sides of my family. I have 2 younger brothers. I am a daughter, a wife, a sister, an aunty, a friend, and a mother of Sachi, who is my dog and the center of my universe, and my cat, Lulu.

I graduated from Mid-Pacific Institute in Honolulu. If you're from Hawaii, you are more than likely familiar with Mid-Pac. My parents had me attend this school primarily because they had dorms so I could reside on the campus while going to school. This gives you an idea of the kind of teenager I was growing up. Invincible in my mind, for sure.

I attended Gonzaga University with ambitions and aspirations of becoming a criminal defense attorney, and I was fully distracted instead by partying and boys. Needless to say, I never finished my college education.

My journey in self-awareness and in the power of thought started in May of 2000, when I was given an opportunity by a good friend, Natasha, to attend the PSI Basic Seminar. Every obstacle I had to not attend she handled, leaving me no back doors. At the time, I was living separate from my second husband and on the brink of another marriage falling apart. Up until this time, my world was, go to work, come home, go to work, come home, go to work, come home. Mediocrity ruled my life then.

After completing all the PSI Seminars curriculum, I started working for PSI Seminars. I worked for that company for a total of 12 years, holding various positions such as the Life Success Course Producer, Women's Leadership Seminar Producer and Advanced Course Manager.

I have been immersed in this work of self-exploration, self-discovery and personal development for 19 years and counting. I've worked with thousands of people, and I continue to work with people in their own self-discovery journey. My own self-discovery is continuous. There is no arrival point that I have found for myself. I intend to keep learning until my last breath. Hear me when I say, it wasn't until I fell completely in love with Kareen, that I was equipped to work with other people to do the same.

It wasn't until I actually hit all those hard truths about myself; it wasn't until I was honest enough and brave enough to say to myself, "This is what is"; it wasn't until those moments, that I actually started loving myself. In loving myself, I then started to love other people—it was definitely an Inside-Out journey. I think that's where we often miss the mark. We're looking for external validation versus validating and assigning our own value to who we are as women.

There's a whole bunch more to Kareen. I love everything that has to do with food. I love animals. I love Hugh Jackman. I love a good cup of coffee. I love making a difference in the world. AND, what I really love most of all, is a woman who is 100% in love with ALL of who she is. There is nothing more beautiful to me on this planet than that.

CHAPTER 2:

My Experiences in Loving Myself

(Subira)

I think it's important to talk about some of the things you've lived through, as you've lived through some amazing life events. What kinds of things have you done and what experiences have you had in loving yourself that are relevant to our audience of women ages 45 and up?

(Kareen)

I'll go back as far as I can recall. I was nine years old when my parents got divorced and my dad left. In that moment, little Kareen had an emotional experience and made up something to match that feeling, which was, "I'm not lovable." As little people, we are not equipped with reason and logic. All we are equipped to do is feel. Little Kareen made up that she was not lovable, because if she were lovable, Dad would have stayed. Fast forward in time, decade after decade after decade, and now I've got all these added sub-categories in addition to the "I'm not lovable" belief, such as, "I don't matter, I'm not important, I'm not special."

When I think about that in real time as an adult, I have three divorces under my belt, and I'm certainly not boasting about it. My point being, as an adult, I started to look at HOW my belief of "I'm not lovable" played itself out, over and over again.

A pivotal part of my journey here was to identify where these beliefs came from that I had about myself, that were not true. This wasn't conscious at all for me. I wasn't moving through my life as an adult, falling in love, saying to my future husbands, "Hey, we're in love, let's get married. Oh, and by the way, I really believe that I'm not lovable, so we are fucked." It was not conscious at all. It was entirely unconscious. That's the stuff. That's the work. That's where the unraveling of all the things I didn't want to look at resided. I didn't want to look at them because they were painful, because they weren't pretty. That's just one example of a belief I had adopted as my own truth that was not true.

At the age of 19, I married for the first time knowing inside my guts that it was a NO. I did not listen to my intuition and married him anyway. For the next seven years, I was abused and beaten physically, mentally and emotionally by this man. Here's the thing: the reason I allowed that behavior in my life was because it matched my own self-assessment. There's no other way I would have allowed it. That's the rub; that's the hard part I didn't want to look at. At first, that was not an easy concept for me to accept and to be with, and the truth is, I don't even recognize that version of me today. I just don't.

I have said yes to job opportunities knowing full well each was a no. I have accepted salary proposals knowing it was beneath my value. I have lived through betrayal and loss. I have recovered from physical pain. I have fallen over and over and over again, only to rise up over and over and over again. Through it all, the fun stuff, the painful stuff, the boxes of tissues and puffy eyes, here I stand, whole, solid, strong, and deeply connected to my vision to speak to women around the world.

(Subira)

Our ego always wants us to be correct. "Hey, my job is to make you right and to save your life." So, little Kareen made up a story at nine that said, "I'm not lovable, which is why Daddy left." Fast forward 10 years: you get married and you're getting this intuitive hit that says, "No." Do you think you were able at 19 to recognize a yes and a no on a visceral level?

(Kareen)

Yes, I do. As I replay that time in my life, I was still living in choices that affirmed "I'm NOT lovable." I attracted him into my life to affirm that belief. The connection to my intuition was there; I just didn't listen to it. What definitely serves me and guides me today is shutting up long enough to actually LISTEN to my intuition.

CHAPTER 3:

Changes Made As A Result Of Loving Myself

(Subira)

What changes have you seen in loving yourself since you started on this path?

(Kareen)

One of my benchmarks was leaving my first marriage filled with abuse. I can vividly recall the moment after we divorced buying myself a pretty dress for the first time in seven years. I was in the dressing room in the store with this pretty dress on, looking at myself in the full-view mirror and sobbing. I was sobbing because for the first time in seven years, I had taken action that affirmed I was worthy, I was important, and I was lovable.

During my attendance of the PSI Basic seminar in May of 2000, there was an exercise called Victim-Responsible. I had to pick a real-life event from the past that I still had energy on, that still evoked an emotional response. I picked my first marriage to use in this exercise. I was to first speak about this as a victim. That was easy. Then, I was to speak the exact life event from the place of responsibility. That was not so easy at the time. However, it was pivotal because only then did I identify that the abuse matched my own self-worth. It was one of the most powerful discoveries I made about myself as it changed forever the value I assigned to myself. I realized that I have the ability to assign my own value and worth to who I am as a woman.

This was not an easy pill to swallow at first. However, the greatest piece on the other side is, I now live in what affirms the following truths: "I matter," "I am important," "I am lovable."

(Subira)

What are some areas where women might see the pattern of "I'm not worthy" showing up?

(Kareen)

I would say, if everyone pays a little bit more attention, it is showing up everywhere. The illusion comes with thinking, I am one way over here at my job, and then I'm this way over here at home. That is an un-truth. Wherever I go, there I am. I can tell you that for me, it has shown up in every facet of my life, in both my relationships and in my career path. For example, I have said yes to job opportunities knowing full well they were NO's. I have accepted salary proposals, knowing full well they were beneath the value I bring. I would feel disgusted and sick every morning, getting up and going to that job that was completely out of alignment with my values. And as you know, I have said YES to relationships, with my insides screaming at me, "NO! NO! NO! Run, Kareen!"

(Subira)

I think that's important for women to understand. I love the way you said, "Wherever you go, there you are." The way it resonates for me is, "The way I do anything, is the way I do everything."

(Kareen)

When I'm not in alignment, it will manifest itself in some way, in my body with something. For me, here's how I check myself. I close my eyes and breathe and notice the following:

Is what I think about, what I speak about, what I feel about and what I do, all the same?

When they are all the same, I know I am in alignment. I also know right away when I am NOT in alignment. I'm either not speaking my truth, or my actions are not honoring myself, etc. When I allow myself to remain out of alignment, it will manifest in illness, pain, disease and turmoil.

CHAPTER 4:

What May Be Unnoticed

(Subira)

What are some subtle or gradual changes you've seen over time that most women 45 and older may not have noticed?

(Kareen)

In my life, one of the greatest changes since I started on this journey, is being in harmony with other women versus being in competition with them. This is huge. First of all, being a woman in this world is complicated at best. It can be confusing if we allow all the external noise to be what we hang our hats on as a guide on how we're supposed to show up as a woman in the world. If we listen to it, it is no mystery how confusing it can all become.

I was born a Japanese American girl. I was supposed to be a boy. Well, I came out a girl, and like I said earlier, I was the first grandchild on both sides. Kind of a double whammy there. I was raised to be in competition with other women. Whether intended or not, that was my life experience growing up.

As women, there's so much competition amongst us. I find this to be more common than not. However, I have found our naturalness is to be in harmony with each other, to raise each other up. In my own journey, until I started to really love me, I could not give it away. I just couldn't; it wasn't possible. At 50, I have created relationships with women in a way that I've never experienced before. I call it "The REAL DEAL uplifting." It is the kind of uplifting where my sister is ALL UP IN MY BUSINESS when I am playing small or self-sabotaging. She literally takes a stand for what it is I say I want. It's the kind of uplifting where my sister reminds me that I am great, I am deserving, I am significant and I matter, especially in the moments when I think I am NOT. She's got my back and my front and will walk with me to my finish line. No one gets to speak poorly about me in her presence—nobody. Remember this, it's not always this woo-woo, feel-good, pompoms and confetti, cheering-for-me thing. Sometimes, it is, "Oh Kareen, put on your big-girl panties and get your ass up off that couch, because you said you were committed to making this happen, today," kind of thing.

It's not the fake and phony. It's not the feel-good stuff all the time. I get to authentically be me in her company as she gets to authentically be her in mine. Within that exchange, we are revealing and sharing the things we hold secret and the things we're ashamed of. Without the relationships I have with other women who hold me up, I could self-sabotage if I wanted to far more easily and readily. I could live underneath who I really am if I wanted to. Right now, I do a damn good job of keeping my line up.

Another change that is apparent is that women are more empowered than ever today. Women are rising and helping each other unlike ever before. The voices of women are being heard, and I feel a responsibility to be a part of it because I am a woman. So, rise up and do it now.

CHAPTER 5:

Challenges Women Face

(Subira)

What do you think the big challenges are that women face right now?

(Kareen)

The answer to the question is separating who you believe you are from who you really are so you can get to authentically loving yourself. In my own journey, my biggest challenge was arriving to the door of LOVING MYSELF by literally severing the beliefs I had of who I thought I was from the realizations of WHO I AM.

After years of physical and emotional abuse, it was time for me to start separating the story I made up about who I believed I was versus who I really am. Who I really am is Magnificent. Who I really am is Deserving. Who I really am is here to make a difference in the world. The two entities: the story I made up about who I am and WHO I REALLY AM, were battling each other. And so, it was time to end that battle.

Hear me when I say, I spent at least 3 decades of my life believing that it would only be a matter of time before someone screwed me over. Then I justified this belief by telling myself that I could get through life without people in it, that I didn't need people, that everyone always wanted something from me, and on and on and on. AND, my life really didn't suck either. Now, the depth of relationships I had in my life then was shallow—ankle-high, at best. No one was granted access to Kareen.

So, the big challenge today, tomorrow, and always is:

Separating who you believe you are from WHO YOU REALLY ARE by your willingness to be HONEST about yourself and with yourself. Honestly acknowledging each and every component of your Point A. Experiencing every joy, sorrow, anger and pain encapsulated within that Point A, will allow the journey forward to your Point B: your vision and your purpose-driven life. I promise. You cannot avoid or deny parts and pieces of that Point A to get there, though. You MUST embrace it ALL.

I think the key you may be searching for to unlock the doorway to your purpose-driven life, your reason for being here and breathing air on the planet, is a key that YOU hold within you. It's not found or attained outside of you. It's such a simple statement: "Love yourself." Okay, great. Well, it's a nice concept, but it's not necessarily an easy process, because within that process, you've got to lift up the carpet and look at all that dirt down there, that you don't want to look at. You've got to stop denying and avoiding those parts of you, the dark side, the shadows—whatever they might be.

What I have found is, they're all one in the same. All my pain is as immense as all my love. All my joy is as immense as all my sorrow. I cannot experience one without the other. They're one in the same. Getting to that place of loving who you are is the most empowering place I know. It is also where my vision was birthed.

What becomes available now is a vision that is bigger than me. It is a vision that is not about me anymore. I don't believe that we're put here for no reason. I don't believe we're here breathing air because there's nothing better to do.

I believe everyone's here for a purpose. Or else, we wouldn't be here. There's a divine gift within each one of us just waiting to be expressed. Let's go express it, and for God's sake, please don't wait till you're 50, like me, to do it. It took me 50 years to get to this point.

(Subira)

So, that sounds like willingness. Can you talk to me a little bit deeper about willingness?

(Kareen)

You know that phrase, "You can lead a horse to water, but you can't make it drink?" You can lead it to water though.

I was certainly led to water over and over and over and over again, and my unwillingness to drink that water, my unwillingness to dive into that pain, to dive into that sorrow and to release myself of all the shame and guilt around whatever I thought I was "supposed" to be and never

24

measured up to, kept me from getting to the other side. The other side is called *loving myself.*

I grew up with the belief that says, "Good women are seen and not heard." Shush your mouth, Kareen, was the message I received.

Well, why do I have a mouth and a voice if that's the case? I really do believe in my heart of hearts that my great grandmother, my grandmother, and my mother ALL did the best they knew how. However, I'm here to stop the cycle of "good women are seen and not heard." I'm here to stop the cycle of "money doesn't grow on trees." I'm here to stop the cycle of all the "shoulds" that have been put upon me as a woman. If it doesn't serve me, if it doesn't empower me, if it doesn't lead me to living my vision, it does not get to pass "Go" and collect $200. They are paradigms that are not even true.

CHAPTER 6:

Big Opportunities Missed

(Subira)

What are the big opportunities women might be missing in loving themselves?

(Kareen)

I think one of the biggest opportunities missed is, we simply don't put ourselves on the list. We don't put ourselves on the calendar of our life. We don't schedule ourselves in. We don't make ourselves important. Women wear many different hats at the same time. The mother hat, the wife hat, the boss hat, the daughter hat, the sister hat, etc. So often, we fail to put on the hat with our own name on it. Often, we will be and do for everyone else in our daily regimen and forget ourselves completely. Schedule yourself on your calendar of your life. Make yourself important. You are not squeezed in because there is an hour remaining in your day. Put yourself on your calendar of your life and allow everything else to be scheduled around YOU. Nobody else can make you important. Only you can do that.

So, put yourself on your calendar, making yourself important because you say so, not because it's convenient, not because, "Oh, the boys are at soccer, so I've got an extra 30 minutes." No, you do it because it's important and you're important. You are NOT an after-thought.

The second thing I definitely can speak to, and it was an opportunity that I certainly missed over and over and over again, because I just wasn't willing to let people in, is to create a tribe of women around me that think I'm the greatest thing since sliced bread. Here's the thing though: I cannot give to my sister what I don't first give to myself. I cannot give out what I do not first put IN. It's an Inside-Out job. You must love and give to you in order to love and give to your sisters. That's the only way it can happen.

Once you make YOU significant, start identifying your tribe of women. These women will match the way you love yourself. They will hold you, love you, give it to you straight, cry with you, belly laugh with you, create and manifest with you, make you a cocktail, eat delicious food with you, and most of all, they will remind you of your purpose-filled vision to be manifested.

There's just something special and different for me as a woman when I allow, create, and nurture these kinds of connections with other women in this way.

CHAPTER 7:

Focus on You

(Subira)

Where do you think women can focus their efforts to experience self-worth and to honor themselves?

(Kareen)

Remember that loving yourself is an Inside-Out job. You got to focus on you. Focus on the inside first. Do you. Put you first. Nothing will be long-lasting and different until it's different and long-lasting in you. Focus on you. Do you. Stay in your lane.

Do not be distracted by people, vibrations, and events that don't match and support what it is you want to make happen for you. Be okay saying no to those people, places and things. I think there's huge power in those two letters, "n" and "o." Use your "no's" and claim your "yes's." You must put you first. It's like putting yourself on the calendar again and creating support in your life.

I always do something that honors my highest and best, every single day.

It doesn't have to be time-consuming. It can be five minutes or it can be an hour. When I'm rolling on three tires because I'm going, going, going, going, and now, I'm running on fumes, to honor myself in those moments, I bring balance back into my life. I turn off the phone, I turn off the computer, I turn off my brain and I take a nap. I do what I need to do to refuel to get that fourth tire back up and running again. Then, I'm able to be of service to myself and to others.

As a result of honoring myself daily, over time, solutions start appearing, opportunities start arriving and visions start emerging. So, DO the things that honor your highest and best.

Do the things that bring harmony and balance into your life. Be purposeful in exercising your mind. Get in alignment. DO the things that ignite your passion, your vision, your purpose. You've got to start somewhere. So, start with a CUP of tea if that blows your skirt up. Make the most delicious cup of tea and enjoy every sip of it.

(Subira)

Today, I went for a walk for an hour, before I give anything to anybody. I walk for me because I like to feel powerful in my body. When I feel strong, I feel like I'm invincible. So, I think it's beautiful to put yourself first; thank you for that.

CHAPTER 8:

Mistakes

(Subira)

Where do you see women 45 and older making mistakes or missing the boat?

(Kareen)

One of the biggest mistakes is thinking that someone else is going to bring you happiness and fulfillment. Only YOU have the power to create your own happiness and fulfillment that is meaningful and long lasting. Everything else is temporary. Again, it is an Inside-Out job.

Another mistake I often see is looking for external validation versus validating our own value.

You know the saying, "What you think of me is none of my business?" Infuse that concept into every cell in your body. We waste so much time caring about what other people think about what we're doing or not doing. Caring about what other people think is a complete waste of time. It doesn't serve us in getting to that purpose-driven life. At the end of the day, if what we're going for is long-lasting fulfillment, seeking external validation is like being on a giant wheel with a dangling carrot that you are constantly and continuously chasing, with absolutely no long-lasting reward.

The only approval you require is your own; you set the stage of your life.

When I got cemented into what my core values were, I was responsible for my own happiness and fulfillment and did not require external validation any longer. Once I did a whole lot of exploration and discovery on me and on the hard truths about what had gotten in the way, about what I allowed and what I actually blocked off, and once I got to that place of loving me, I became cemented in my non-negotiable values.

Those values have certainly shifted and changed as I have shifted and changed. What was important to me 20 years ago isn't even important now.

These values are non-wavering. They're non-negotiables, and they're literally the values that I am willing to stake my life on. Out of that, I can tell you that there were real-life moments when I was standing alone in those values, and they weren't easy moments necessarily. Some of my family members weren't coming with me in those values. Friends of many years were not coming with me in those values. Yet, like the rudder on the ship, they guide every choice I make, and they stand me straight up over and over again.

CHAPTER 9:

Speak Your Truth

(Subira)

What are some major events or developments that you see in the immediate future for women when it comes to loving themselves?

(Kareen)

There are more women speakers now than ever before, speaking their truths and delivering their messages to the world. I find this to be a huge development as they inspire me to go out and speak my divine message, as well. I do believe we're seeing more and more women creating their own unique platforms, impacting the world. I certainly identify with women who are speaking on certain topics currently. There are female speakers who are emerging right now, and I think out of that, what happens is other women are being inspired to speak their message and their purpose.

I lived so long believing that I was an isolated island, and I was completely disconnected to other people in the world. I actually believed that I could live my life separate from everybody. It's simply not true. What is true is we are all connected.

Every time a woman has the courage to speak her truth, it inspires me to do the same thing. She is a living example that my voice matters because she made her voice matter. As women emerge and speak their voices, it's going to ripple out and it's going to touch other women. As a result of that, we are going to touch each other. So globally, I believe this connection and inspiration will not just be on the home front, not only affecting mothers with their children. It's going to be in the workforce, on the stages, on the platforms where there are women. Being willing to be honest, honest with me first, honest with you next, creates something that wasn't present before.

That's energetic to me, and it's felt. Every time I raise up somebody else, I'm simply raising myself up too. As women start rising up, and as they start speaking their voices and sharing their stories, I do believe "IT" will touch us all. It's like it starts to rain down upon us. Wherever a woman is standing, whether it's in our homes or whether it's in the workforce, we will be touched and inspired by her.

CHAPTER 10:

Resources for Loving Yourself

(Subira)

What are some "loving yourself" tools and resources?

(Kareen)

There are so many different vehicles within the personal growth field and mindset training field. All of it is accessible via the internet in this digital world. Because every person is unique and different, certain platforms are going to resonate with certain people. Find what resonates for you, get on that train, and RIDE IT. Ride it until it no longer fits, and then find another vehicle that does fit. The key is to keep on RIDING, so you can keep on learning and growing.

I recommend: PSI Seminars, The Hoffman Institute, Dr. John DeMartini, Mike Dooley, Iyanla Vanzant, Jen Sincero, Mel Robbins, Brene Brown, just to name a few.

Find what speaks to your heart. Find what actually lifts you up and lights you up, and then dive into everything that's available there and soak it all in like a sponge. Actually make things happen in your life, and do it over and over and over again. Learning is never going to end unless you want it to. So, I say, keep learning. In this journey, education is vast, and we are living in this gigantic classroom called planet Earth. I'm learning from every person I encounter, every single one.

CHAPTER 11:

Who Do I Pay Attention to?

(Subira)

Who are the big players women should pay attention to when it comes to loving themselves?

(Kareen)

My first hit to that is pay attention to you. Always and forevermore, we get to know exactly what we're committed to and what we value based on the result that is in front of us in our life. That's truth. Pay attention to you. Be honest with you. No matter how painful, no matter how many tissues you use in a moment, just be honest with you, because from that place, I promise (I'm living proof) that you will be empowered in a whole new and different way as a result of being honest about you, with you. Pay attention to you. Focus on you. Stay in your lane. There's no one who is going to make you matter, except you.

Also, pay attention to the women who are playing big in your hometown and around the globe. Pay attention to the women who are deliberately lifting up other women to their greatness. Pay attention to the women who have released all shame and guilt around expectations on how they are to be in the world. Pay attention to the women who honor their no's and claim their yes's. Pay attention to the young ladies and how you are influencing and impacting their future women selves. Pay attention to the execution of your purpose-driven life.

CHAPTER 12:

What's Important

(Subira)

Is there anything else you think is important and want to share?

(Kareen)

Yes, what I find incredibly important is you and me, in this conversation we are having right now. Every time a woman has the guts to be authentic, real, and genuine in her expression, she not only affirms her own worth, but she also affirms the value in other women too.

I do believe that it is our job as women to bring our wholeness, our divine-ness to everything we do and to every person we touch because we are profoundly amazing. Who you are matters. What you have to say is important. What you have to contribute is significant. We have the ability to actually manifest things that are bigger than we can even imagine in this moment.

There is no life event from your past, in the present, or in the future that is bigger than WHO YOU ARE. You are bigger than every limiting belief you may have about yourself. You are bigger than every tragedy, every heartache, and any loss. You are still standing, reading this book, because what you want is awaiting your arrival.

The only person who can sustain, fulfill, nurture and create your purpose-driven life is YOU. At the end of the day, I always ask myself, "Kareen, can you lay your head down for the day, knowing you did your best?" And in answering myself, I think about these things. Was I kinder today than I was the day before? Did I take things less personally today than I did the day before? Did I take action today in honoring my highest and best? And guess what, I do lay my head down for the day, smiling.

The other thing too, I can tell you for sure, is there was a point in my life when mediocrity ruled my life. All I did was get up, go to work, come home, get up, go to work, come home. I kept hitting repeat.

The pulse of my life was a flat straight line. There were no peaks, there were no valleys, there were no ups, there were no downs and there was no excitement, no purpose and no passion. One of the most dangerous places any human being can live in is in mediocrity. FIND YOUR PASSION!

CHAPTER 13:

Summation

(Subira)

How would you sum up everything we have discussed today to your readers?

(Kareen)

I have two things. The first thing comes from one of my mentors, Ernestine. She would always say to me, "Kareen, remember that every woman we meet can do something better than you and I, even if it's threading a needle."

THIS is where I am no better than she is. THIS is where I learn from her. THIS is where I seek to understand her. THIS is where I become better from knowing her. It's been an invaluable way to be with myself and with other women.

The second message I have is this question: *"If my only job for being here on the planet is to BE the best example of HOW the world is to LOVE ME, how would I be treating myself differently?"*

(Subira)

That is powerful. That is a jewel. Say it again.

(Kareen)

"If my only job for being here on this planet is to BE the best example of HOW the world is to LOVE ME, how would I be treating myself differently?"

(Subira)

I want to be there when you ask that question to a group of women from stage. I know that's going to slay the audience.

Thank you so much for this heartfelt interview. I'm sure you will have an impact on all the women who come in contact with your book. I really want to thank you for showing up so authentically with such an open heart and for speaking from your intuition. Just to watch you close your eyes and go within and speak your truth from this natural place was beautiful, and I'm so honored to be on the other side listening and holding space for you. And to all the women who are reading this book, thank you for joining us in this amazing conversation.

Again, we are talking about the current State of Affairs for women in loving themselves and in empowering themselves. *"To remind and affirm for women that they are bigger than any life event, any belief that they may have about themselves, that has disallowed the full authentic expression of WHO THEY ARE."* These are Kareen's words, not mine.

You, sister, are bigger than any life event, indeed.

Thank you for offering your experience and love, and I look forward to your next offering.

You may contact the author directly at lovingyourself247@gmail.com, as well as visit her website, www.kareenborzone.com.

RESOURCES

National Crisis Organization and Assistance

The National Domestic Violence Hotline

1-800-799-7233 (SAFE)

www.ndvh.org

National Dating Abuse Hotline

1-866- 331-9474

www.loveisrespect.org

Americans Overseas Domestic Violence Crisis Center

International toll-free (24/7)

1-866-USWOMEN (879 - 6636)

www.86uswomen.org

National Sexual Assault Hotline

1-800-656-4673 (HOPE)

www.rainn.org

National Suicide Prevention Lifeline

1-800-273-8255 (TALK)

www.suicidepreventionlifeline.org

Legal

American Bar Association Commission on Domestic & Sexual Violence

1-202-662-1000

www.abanet.org/domviol

Battered Women's Justice Project

1-800-903-0111

www.bwjp.org

Legal Momentum

1-212-925-6635

www.legalmomentum.org

Womenslaw.org

www.womenslaw.org

National Clearinghouse for the Defense of Battered Women

1-800-903-0111, ext. 3

www.ncdbw.org